CONFRONTING RUSSIA'S WEAPONIZATION OF INFORMATION

HEARING

BEFORE THE

COMMITTEE ON FOREIGN AFFAIRS
HOUSE OF REPRESENTATIVES

ONE HUNDRED FOURTEENTH CONGRESS

FIRST SESSION

APRIL 15, 2015

Serial No. 114–37

Printed for the use of the Committee on Foreign Affairs

Available via the World Wide Web: http://www.foreignaffairs.house.gov/ or
http://www.gpo.gov/fdsys/

U.S. GOVERNMENT PUBLISHING OFFICE

94–186PDF   WASHINGTON : 2015

For sale by the Superintendent of Documents, U.S. Government Publishing Office
Internet: bookstore.gpo.gov   Phone: toll free (866) 512–1800; DC area (202) 512–1800
Fax: (202) 512–2104   Mail: Stop IDCC, Washington, DC 20402–0001

CONTENTS

CONFRONTING RUSSIA'S WEAPONIZATION OF INFORMATION

WEDNESDAY, APRIL 15, 2015

HOUSE OF REPRESENTATIVES,
COMMITTEE ON FOREIGN AFFAIRS,
Washington, DC.

The committee met, pursuant to notice, at 10 o'clock a.m., in room 2172 Rayburn House Office Building, Hon. Edward Royce (chairman of the committee) presiding.

Chairman ROYCE. This hearing will come to order. I will ask if the members can all take their seats.

And I had an opportunity in the early 1980s to go into East Germany and spend some time there, and during that time to see the quality of propaganda being broadcast into the East Bloc by Russia, the type of disinformation campaign that was going on.

And I would have to say that since that time the caliber of propaganda has become much more clever than that which was disseminated then.

And today we are going to look at the danger of Russia's misinformation campaign in Europe and, indeed, today that misinformation campaign is worldwide and we are also going to look at the failed response to that effort.

And as we will hear today, Russia's propaganda machine is really at this time in overdrive and part of the focus, from my standpoint, seems to be to subvert democratic stability. And, frankly, there is also an element of this that goes to the issue of fomenting violence in Eastern Europe.

Now, myself and Eliot Engel had an opportunity to go into Dnepropetrovsk and talk to civil society, the women's groups, a lot of different organizations, the lawyers groups, and this was one of the issues that people are concerned about and these tactics have undermined the government in Ukraine and, frankly, helped lay a foundation for invasion there.

This same plan is being worked in Eastern and Central Europe and this Russian propaganda has the potential to destabilize NATO members and it could impact our security commitments, es-pecially if we look at some of what is going on in the Baltic States. So this Russian campaign, what one witness describes as the "weaponization of information," seriously threatens U.S. security.

Russia has deployed an information army inside television, radio, and newspapers throughout Europe.

Some are doing the Kremlin's bidding and are given explicit guidelines to obscure the truth by spreading conspiracies, and I

(1)

would just give you examples of some of the things you read now on these Russian broadcasts or some of the things that are alluded to.

One was a conspiracy that our own Government here is responsible for everything from 9/11, the attack on 9/11 to the downing of Malaysia Flight MH17 over Ukraine. Others are simply paid more for demonizing the West, while those who pursue credible reporting are pushed aside.

Today, we will hear from journalist Liz Wahl, who dramatically interrupted a live broadcast to resign from RT, a Russian outlet, explaining she could not stand by its distorted coverage of Russia's occupation of Ukraine.

Meanwhile, independent journalists in Russia have come under attack. There have been three journalists in Russia killed so far this year. Unfortunately, Ms. Wahl is a rarity.

So Russian speakers in the frontline states like the Baltic, Ukraine, and Moldova continue to be told that their governments want to oppress and render them second class citizens.

Unfortunately, many are buying this divisive message. In parts of Europe where there aren't Russian speaking populations there is also a message and that message is that Western democracy is morally corrupt and that integration with Europe since the Cold War has failed.

It is estimated that Putin is spending more than $600 million a year to deride democratic pluralism and the U.S. response to this? Well, the agency expected to manage our response, the Broadcasting Board of Governors, is far behind.

After years of Mr. Putin ramping up the effort in Russia, last fall the BBG finally launched its flagship response to Russian propaganda—a mere 30-minute television news program in the Russian language called "Current Time."

The program was put on air in Lithuania, Moldova, Georgia, Ukraine, and Latvia. But after just 4 months it was pulled in Latvia because it couldn't draw an audience. Now, what U.S.-backed news and information that does get through, the amount of that is a thimble of journalistic credibility in an ocean of Russian-driven news distortion and this isn't a matter of resources, from my perspective.

U.S. broadcasters are laboring under a flawed bureaucracy. Members may recall that then Secretary Clinton called the agency defunct in her testimony before this committee in 2013.

The Inspector General and the Government Accountability Office have been highly critical, and the agency hired a CEO and he quit after 42 days on the job. Last week, the director of the VOA announced his resignation.

Our international broadcasting is in disarray. The journalists of the BBG risk their lives reporting from the front lines across the world. They deserve better support, and the American people need much more from this agency if we are going to respond to the rapidly evolving media environment and better secure the long-term security interests of the United States.

Last Congress, the House unanimously passed bipartisan legislation introduced by myself and Ranking Member Eliot Engel. This legislation is referenced in an op-ed today in the Wall Street Journal that I wrote.

But I will just share with the members here that that legislation will help us fight Putin's propaganda by allowing more resources to be spent in the field and on content instead of on a broken bureaucracy, and by clarifying the BBG's mission, creating accountable leadership through a CEO and reducing the bureaucracy, this can lead to a situation where the budget there can be spent on disseminating truthful news and that should be the goal.

Righting international broadcasting must be an urgent priority in our foreign policy, and now I would like to turn to the ranking member of this committee and the co-author of the legislation to do this, Mr. Eliot Engel of New York.

Mr. ENGEL. Thank you very much, Mr. Chairman.

Thank you for calling this morning's hearing and I especially want to thank you for your leadership as this committee works to address the growing Russian threat. You have really been right on top of it.

I really appreciate it and it is just so important. Thank you for your courage and for your voice. It has been a pleasure to be your partner.

Let me also thank our witnesses today for sharing your expertise about a major part of that threat—Russia's new and intensified propaganda effort.

It is long past due that we take a hard look at this challenge. The Kremlin's disorientation campaign goes beyond political spin and disinformation.

What we see pouring out of the Kremlin amounts to the weaponization of information. Propaganda is a critical element of Russia's so-called hybrid warfare strategy, a strategy on devastating display in occupied Crimea and war-torn eastern Ukraine.

Coupled with cyber-attacks and other covert operations, these new capabilities and Vladimir Putin's belligerence pose a direct threat to our allies and our interests.

These measures are well financed, these measures are working and these measures demand a robust response from us. Kremlin-controlled media are putting down roots around the world.

Russian financial support is bolstering fringe political parties, creating puppet NGOs and fostering a facade of academic research sympathetic to Vladimir Putin's anti-democratic world view.

The Kremlin aims to undermine democratic organizations and alliances. Russia's leaders want to divide allies and partners while seeking to discredit the post-Cold War order in Europe.

This strategy is not just to disseminate lies but to sow doubt and confusion, especially about what is actually and really happening in Ukraine. The component of this propaganda war that concerns me most is the influx of Kremlin-controlled television broadcasts in frontline states.

From the Baltics to Central Asia, a Russian-speaking population of nearly 100 million people is getting its news from such distorted broadcasts. Here, the Kremlin uses high quality entertainment to draw an audience, then interlaces that programming with their twisted and false perspective on political, military and economic events.

Today, I hope we can hear more about Russia's propaganda campaign and, more importantly, what we can do to push back against it. We cannot match the hundreds of millions of dollars the Kremlin is blowing into this effort.

Instead, we must look to create thinking and broad-based partnerships. Given the scale of the Kremlin efforts, it is clear to me that traditional public affairs and public diplomacy, while important parts of a broader effort, do not go far enough.

We have seen some promising initiatives. For instance, the Governments of Latvia and Estonia are developing a plan to launch Russian language television networks in their respective countries.

They want to create platform for content sharing and establish a fund for the production of locally focused content. Additionally, we anticipate a feasibility study this spring from the European Endowment for Democracy recommending a similar approach.

Mr. Chairman, as you recognized, the United States needs its own strategy to deal with this and we need it now. I have been told that our State Department is now working full tilt toward a plan to address this problem.

This can't come soon enough. We are eager to work with the administration to develop this plan and set it in motion because the United States has a major role to play.

In my view, the United States is in a unique position to convene partners from the private sector that will be essential for the success of such initiatives. Furthermore, U.S. leadership will be necessary to ensuring that reluctant Western European allies understand and appreciate the risks posed by an unchecked Kremlin propaganda campaign.

One thing is clear. Meeting this challenge will certainly not be easy. A nondemocratic government in Russia is able to devote nearly limitless resources to spreading lies and sowing confusion, disinformation and division.

But the stakes are high and acting sooner rather than later will make a daunting task a little easier and much more effective over the long run.

I look forward to hearing our witnesses' views on this challenge and their ideas about how we are going to deal with it. So thank you again, Mr. Chairman, for calling this hearing.

Chairman ROYCE. Thank you, Mr. Engel.

We will begin with Mr. Peter Pomerantsev. He is the senior fellow to the Transitions Forum at the Legatum Institute in London.

His writing focuses largely on 21st century propaganda. It is featured regularly in the London Review of Books and the Atlantic Financial Times in foreign policy and elsewhere. He is author of the "The Menace of Unreality: How the Kremlin Weaponizes Information, Culture and Money."

We will hear next from Ms. Elizabeth Wahl. She formally worked for the U.S. Branch of RT Television until her resignation last year on live Russian television in protest to President Putin's government and their distorted coverage of the conflict in Eastern Europe. Ms. Wahl is now a freelance journalist and public speaker.

Ms. Helle Dale is the senior fellow in public diplomacy studies for the Heritage Foundation where her work focuses on the U.S.

Government's institutions and programs for strategic outreach to the public of foreign countries.

Ms. Dale's career started in journalism where she worked for both domestic and foreign publications as well as print and electronic media.

And I would also like to welcome the Vaclav Havel Journalism Fellowship Program, an initiative of Radio Free Europe, Russia Liberty and the Ministry of Foreign Affairs of the Czech Republic. The Vaclav Havel journalism fellows in attendance today, and they are in the second row there on the left, are from Belarus, from Moldova, Ukraine, Georgia, and Russia who have been targeted, these particular journalists have been targeted by the Kremlin and have been victims of Putin's assault on free media, and we thank them for being with us here today.

And without objection, the witnesses' full prepared statements will be made part of the record and members will have 5 calendar days to submit statements and questions and any extraneous material for the record.

And so I would encourage you, Mr. Pomerantsev, if you would like to summarize your remarks for 5 minutes lay out the case.

Then we will go to Ms. Wahl and Helle Dale and then we will go to our members for questions.

STATEMENT OF MR. PETER POMERANTSEV, SENIOR FELLOW, THE LEGATUM INSTITUTE

Mr. POMERANTSEV. Thank you very much for having me here.

Russia's information war—we have been hearing these words a lot lately. Russia has launched the most amazing information warfare blitzkrieg we have ever seen since Supreme Allied Commander General Philip Breedlove after the annexation of Crimea.

We are losing the information war, complained the British head of the House of Commons' Culture and Media Committee as the Kremlin international media was launched in London.

Information war is now the main type of war, argues Dmitry Kiselyov, the infamous Russian TV presenter and Kremlin media boss who also likes to remind the world, and it shows, that Russia can turn the USA into radioactive ash. But what do we mean when we say information war?

Because if we mean propaganda as mass persuasion, propaganda in the sense of some sort of geopolitical debate where each side tries to convince the other it is right, well, then we don't understand the real threat of the Kremlin's information war at all.

To understand what it actually is, let us go back to 1999. Back then, Russian Defense Minister Marshal Igor Sergeyev admitted the Kremlin could never match the West militarily and needed to find, in his words, revolutionary powers and asymmetric responses to compete.

Look at it from the Kremlin's point of view. NATO is undefeatable on the battlefield. The West has a much stronger social and political system—democracy based on openness and competition.

But what if the Kremlin could bypass NATO militarily, make war without ever, officially at least, firing a shot? What if it could use the very openness of democracy's open markets, open culture and, very importantly, open information against us?

So over the 21st century, Russian military theorists developed a theory of what they called information psychological or hybrid war—a mix of media, economic and cultural warfare with a dab of covert military action.

We saw an early example of this is Estonia in 2007 when Estonian authorities decided to move a Soviet war memorial from the center of the city. Russian media, which is very widely available in Estonia, went into a frenzy, accusing the Estonians of fascism.

Russian vigilante groups started riots in the center of Tallinn. A massive cyber-attack disabled Estonia's Government and banking sectors.

Moscow was sending a message, despite membership of NATO and EU, that Estonia and all other frontline states were still vulnerable and the Kremlin could cripple them without giving Estonia a chance to invoke NATO's Article 5.

The aim was not just to humiliate Tallinn but show that Western and, specifically, American promises of security are empty and once the NATO alliance has been undermined and American influence weakened, then the Kremlin will have a stronger hand to play around the world.

Since 2007, the Kremlin's information psychological strategy has expanded. The Kremlin is now bankrolling and lending political support to both far right and far left parties in Europe while using open markets to make whole countries dependent on its money and energy.

Unlike their Soviet predecessors, this regime will work with anyone as long as they help create stability in their home countries. The Kremlin is also putting out its message in multiple media 24/7.

Russian language media reaches 30 million Russians outside of Russia, a lot of them in EU and NATO states. The Kremlin has invested hundreds of millions into foreign language media.

Russia Today (RT) broadcasts in English, Spanish, German and Arabic. There is the web and radio service Sputnik, while the Kremlin also funds troll farms, regime-funded companies who spread messages online in social media and comment sections.

Conspiracy theories, disinformation and fake news are a staple in these media claims that the U.S. invented Ebola as a weapon or re-editing interviews with Ukrainian rabbis to make it seem contrary to what they actually said, that there is a threat to the Jewish community in post-Maidan Ukraine, or even planting stories that the Rand Corporation is advising the Ukrainian Government on how to ethnically cleanse east Ukraine.

The ultimate aim of the Kremlin's international media is not to make anyone like Russia. It is not PR or necessarily engaged in fact-based journalism.

Instead, information is used to sow divisions, demoralize and disorganize—to weaponize information. After Malaysian Flight MH-17 was shot down over eastern Ukraine by Russian missiles last summer, Russian media spewed out scores of outlandish stories, blaming Ukrainian fighter jets, claiming the plane had deliberately taken off from Amsterdam carrying dead bodies.

Their aim appears to have been to trash the information space with so much misinformation that a conversation based on actual facts would become impossible. This is not merely an information war but a war on information.

If the very possibility of rational argument is submerged in a fog of uncertainty, the public will give up trying to understand what happened. Trust, the key ingredient of democracy, is destroyed and the strategy is working.

Recent research in Ukraine and the Baltics shows that audiences exposed to both Russian and local media end up not trusting anyone. In Germany, 43 percent do not trust anything they read on Ukraine.

Throughout Europe, conspiracy theories are on the rise and in the U.S. trust in the media has declined. The Kremlin may not always have initiated this phenomena but it is fanning them.

And I would like to finish with the fact it is not just Russia and the Kremlin doing it. The Chinese are starting a similar tactic in Asia. We see how ISIS works in the Middle East.

This is a global problem. Thank you.

[The prepared statement of Mr. Pomerantsev follows:]

Peter Pomeranzev

Senior Fellow, Legatum Institute

House Committee on Foreign Affairs

April 15 2014, 'Confronting Russia's Weaponization of Information'

During the Russian invasion of Crimea last year, most of the world's journalists seemed confused. Most of the West's leaders were taken aback. But when it was over, the Supreme Allied Commander Europe (SACEUR), General Philip M. Breedlove, defined what had happened very precisely. The Kremlin had launched "the most amazing information warfare blitzkrieg we have ever seen in the history of information warfare'. To put it differently, Russia has launched an information war against the West – and we are losing.

Crimea was the culmination of a long process, not the beginning. The Kremlin's military theorists have long been preparing to fight what they call 'information-psychological war', a mix of media, psychological, economic and cultural warfare. We saw an early example of these tactics in Estonia in 2007. When Estonian authorities decided to move a Soviet war memorial from the center of the city, Russian media went into a frenzy, accusing the Estonians of fascism. Russian vigilante groups started riots in the center of Tallinn. A massive cyber attack disabled Estonia's government and banking sectors. Moscow was sending a message: despite its membership of NATO and the EU, Estonia was still vulnerable, and the Kremlin could cripple it even before Estonia had a chance to invoke NATO's Article 5.

Ultimately the aim was not just to humiliate Tallinn, but show that Western, and specifically American, promises of security are empty. And once the NATO alliance has been undermined and American influence weakened, then the Kremlin will have a stronger hand to play – economically, politically, culturally - in Europe and around the world.

Since 2007 the Kremlin's information-psychological strategy has indeed expanded. The Kremlin is now bankrolling and lending political support to both far-right and far-left parties in Europe. Unlike their Soviet predecessors, this regime will work with anyone as long as its agenda helps creates instability. Its aim is not to persuade anyone Russia is 'right'. Their aim is to disorganize and demoralize the West.

The Kremlin is also putting out its message in multiple media, 24/7. Russian media directly reaches some 30 million Russians outside the country, in Nato countries such as Estonia and Latvia as well as Ukraine. The Kremlin has also invested hundreds of millions of dollar into foreign language media, including the multilingual news channel RT, or Russia Today, which reaches millions of watchers in English, Spanish, German and Arabic, just for a start. In addition, the Kremlin funds Sputnik, a website news service and radio channel, in many languages. The Kremlin also funds "troll farms," regime-funded companies which hire people to spread messages on social media, using Facebook, Twitter, newspaper comment sections and many other spaces. Through these networks, Russia propagates conspiracy theories, disinformation and fake news. After the Malaysian flight MH17 was shot down over eastern Ukraine with Russian missiles last summer, Russian media spewed out scores of outlandish stories, alternately blaming Ukrainian fighter jets and NATO, and at one point claiming that the plane had deliberately taken off from Amsterdam carrying dead bodies. Their aim was not so much to persuade a potential viewer of any one version, but to trash the information space with so much disinformation so that a conversation based on actual facts would become impossible.

This is not merely an 'information war', in other words, but a 'war on information'. If the very possibility of rational argument is submerged in a fog of uncertainty, there are no grounds for debate. Sooner or later, public will give up trying to understand what happened, or even bothering to listen.

This strategy is working. Recent research by independent NGOs shows that audiences exposed to both Russian and Ukrainian media end up not trusting anyone, the same trend in the Baltic states. In Germany 43 % do not trust anything that they read in Ukraine. Throughout Europe conspiracy theories are on the rise and in the US trust in the media has declined. The Kremlin may not always have initiated these phenomena, but it is fanning them.

In this effort, Russia is not acting alone. The Kremlin is now partnering up with other anti-Western regimes to create international networks of information-psychological operations. RT shares stories with Assad's Syrian TV, and is rebroadcasting with the Argentine state broadcaster. Other rising authoritarian states and non-state actors are developing their own versions of information-psychological war. ISIS' use of media has transformed the Middle East. China is also using a mix of media, legal and psychological warfare to stamp its authority in Asia. In the 21st century the question of whose story wins can be more important than the question of whose army wins.

Democracies are singularly ill equipped to deal with this type of warfare. For all of its military might, NATO cannot fight an information war. The openness of democracies, the very quality that is meant to make them more competitive than authoritarian models, becomes a vulnerability.

But we are not powerless, and we can fight back. If the United States and its allies finally agree to focus on this problem, to treat it with the seriousness it deserves, then there are many options. I hope in today's discussion to elaborate further, but here are some thoughts to begin with.

1. **Defend our information space:** the Kremlin's strategy is not so much an information war as a 'war on information'. During the Ukraine we have seen the importance of NGOs such as Stop Fake in Ukraine, the Interpreter in the US and Belingcat in the UK who expose Kremlin disinformation and launch open-source investigations into such events as the downing of flight MH17. These should be supported, and can

coordinate with each other to form international networks of critical inquiry.

2. **Develop media literacy:** You can't stop disinformation but you can teach people to be more critically aware of how they are being manipulated. Media literacy should be prioritized in education, in the West and beyond.

3. **Anti-corruption networks:** The Kremlin's information-psychological operations often rely on murky funding and corruption to co-opt foreign actors. Journalists and activists should be trained and funded to investigate this world. Currently there are brave groups working independently in various countries, but little coordination. Those investigating corruption need to be protected by a legal fund so they are not intimidated by threats of libel, and need to have the ability to launch their own political lobbying and legal campaigns against the perpetrators. **Research isn't enough: action needs to be enabled, a cross of investigative journalism, activism and legal work.**

4. **Support quality journalism in Central and Eastern Europe:** The West pulled out of media development in Eastern Europe too early. In countries such as Moldova or Ukraine there is no strong quality journalism: media is controlled and manipulated by politicians and oligarchs. In the absence of a beacon of quality journalism, the national conversation disintegrates and a foreign state like Russia can easily spread information chaos. We should support the building up of public broadcasting in the region, rigorously independent of both state and oligarchical influence.

5. **Support independent Russian media through production companies that create new content the Kremlin avoids:** The Kremlin's media operations are impressive but have an Achilles heel. Russia news media virtually ignores 'local news': preferring to distract viewers with the war in Ukraine. This leaves a gap. For local news, and for shows akin to PBS' 'This American Life' or investigations like 'Serial', engaging the Russian language viewer by seeing the world through their eyes. This is a deeper way of projecting democratic values than superficial 're-branding' of the US or 'the West'. The Kremlin wants a PR war. What it is bad at is media that deals with reality.

6. Help Russians with an alternative vision for their country:

The Kremlin defines Russia as at war with the rest of the world. But many Russians have an alternative vision of their country integrated into the international community. Creating a world class Russian university abroad that could foster these values is a way to nurture this vision. One of the many weaknesses of the Kremlin is its failure to support Russian education- putting the lie to its 'great power' propaganda drive.

Most important, it is important for the USG to realize that the 21st century will be defined by new forms of information conflict. A comprehensive approach is urgently needed to deal with this- the West, including the US, is behind the curve.

———

Chairman ROYCE. Thank you.
Ms. Wahl.

STATEMENT OF MS. ELIZABETH WAHL, FORMER RT ANCHOR, FREELANCE JOURNALIST/PUBLIC SPEAKER

Ms. WAHL. All right. We are dealing with an organization that doesn't play by the rules, where the facts on the ground and the reality that citizens face as a result of them don't matter, at least when that reality clashes with Russia's foreign policy agenda.

In that case, one or more alternative realities are pushed, anything to deflect from the facts and confuse the public.

Of course, Russia has a history rich in propaganda but for a while it seemed to lie dormant as many hoped that a reset in diplomatic relations meant a change in direction.

But during the war in Ukraine, the Russian-funded television channel RT was mobilized as a weapon to manipulate people into believing half-truths and lies skewing reality in the Kremlin's favor.

And I saw firsthand how this was orchestrated. When the protests erupted in Maidan Square it was made to look not like a popular uprising but comprised mostly of bloodthirsty neo-Nazis and fascists.

Through misleading language, RT pinned the blame on the West for fomenting unrest in Ukraine. When Russian troops invaded Crimea, Russian media looked the other way. Even Western media organizations indirectly gave strength to Russia's denials in the struggle to maintain balance amid the confusion.

But behind the deliberately confusing rhetoric were essential facts. Russia had invaded a sovereign country and was lying about it. And when it became impossible to deny the presence of what later became known as the little green men, they were hailed as volunteers compelled to rescue fellow Russians from Ukrainian fascists.

Through denial and deception, the Kremlin was able to shape reality or at least make it difficult to uncover what that reality really is. With the international community stunned and incapacitated, Russia sent in tanks, troops and weapons.

Crimea was annexed and Russian-backed separatists gained ground in eastern Ukraine. The disinformation tactics employed by RT during the war in Ukraine I saw used before, though not as vigorously and strategically.

The most celebrated host at the channel holds staunch anti-Western views where deranged conspiracy theories are given a platform. It didn't matter how credible the voices were as long as the underlying message was reinforced—that the U.S. and West is crumbling, corrupt and hypocritical.

There was a running joke among some employees about adopting this mind set by drinking the Kool-Aid. I saw how employees and viewers eventually drank it all up. It is the result of being engrossed in an environment where hating America was rewarded.

It is a mentality that is perpetuated by Internet personalities that gain followers and a sense of belonging by spewing hate and twisting the truth. One of the many things I came to find troubling was the surprising amount of people prone to being manipulated.

Part of it is that with this explosion of information constantly generated online it had become difficult to tell fact from fiction, to sift through it all. Another part of it is the trend of thinking it is hip to believe in any anti-establishment alternative theory.

Russia is aware of this population of paranoid skeptics and plays them like a fiddle. Those that challenge any narrative against Russia are branded CIA agents, of being puppets for neo-conservatives intent on reigniting a cold war and face the ire of seemingly countless paid and volunteer online trolls.

I was accused of being all of these things and faced the constant stream of cyber hate for being perceived as such. Now, this is just a minor example of this new propaganda technique in action.

The Russian bosses say that the organization is simply providing another perspective, one that is ignored in Western media. The implication there is that there is no such thing as an objective truth. But let us not get duped by this falsehood. Someone is responsible for pulling the trigger that killed Russian opposition leader Boris Nemtsov. Someone is responsible for launching the BUK missile that downed MH–17, killing all 298 passengers on board.

This is not open to interpretation because behind the strategically false finger pointing there is a true story and in both cases the story is still unclear and there is someone that prefers it stays that way.

We shouldn't let it slide. We need to take notice and take action and the best weapon against this rapidly expanding propaganda campaign is the truth. We just need to fight for it.

We fight it by refusing to look the other way when a lie is told and by spreading awareness about this new disinformation stream that is polluting the airwaves and online discussions that shape our perception of world events.

We fight it by thinking before clicking, tweeting or sharing an article that aims to deceive, and while it is true that the truth can be difficult to uncover, we should seek to find it, spread it and learn from it whatever that truth may be.

[The prepared statement of Ms. Wahl follows:]

Elizabeth Wahl
Former RT Anchor
Freelance Journalist/Public Speaker
House Committee on Foreign Affairs
April 15, 2015
"Confronting Russia's Weaponization of Information"

We are dealing with an organization that does not play by the rules. Where the facts on the ground and the reality that citizens face as a result of them do not matter - at least when that reality clashes with Russia's foreign policy agenda. In that case, an alternative reality is pushed, or in most cases, several alternative realities - anything to deflect from the facts and confuse the public.

Of course, Russia has a history rich in propaganda. We are well aware of the role it played in the Soviet Era. But for a while, it seemed to lie dormant as many hoped that a reset in diplomatic relations meant a change in direction. But a new propaganda campaign emerged with slick graphics and a seemingly keen resemblance to Western media. During the war in Ukraine, the Russian-funded television channel RT was mobilized as a propaganda tool. It was used as weapon to manipulate people into believing half-truths and lies, skewing reality in the Kremlin's favor.

I saw firsthand how this was orchestrated. When protests erupted in Maiden Square, it was made to look not like a popular uprising, but a coup comprised mostly of bloodthirsty neo-Nazis and fascists. Through suggestive and misleading language, RT pinned the blame on the West for fomenting unrest in Ukraine. When Russian troops invaded Crimea, Russian media looked the other way, playing into the Kremlin's denials. These denials were given credence not only in Russian-funded media, but Western media organizations that indirectly gave strength to Russia's lies for the sake of balance. It became a game of he said, she said: the West is saying this, Russia is saying that. But behind the deliberately confusing rhetoric, were essential facts. Russia invaded a sovereign country and lied about it. When it became impossible to deny the presence of what later became known as the "little green men," they were dubbed "self-defense forces" or volunteers compelled to help out fellow Russians being oppressed by the fascists in Ukraine. Through denial, deception, omission of critical facts, conspiracy theories, and outright lies, Russia was able to shape reality or at least make it difficult to find out what the reality is. With the international community stunned and incapacitated, Russia sent in tanks, troops, and weapons. Crimea was annexed and Russian-backed separatists gained ground in Eastern Ukraine.

The themes and disinformation tactics employed by RT during the war in Ukraine have been used before, though not as vigorously and strategically. The most celebrated hosts at the station held staunch anti-Western views. Conspiracy theories are given a platform at the channel, along with guests with viewpoints that range from unconventional to deranged. It didn't matter how credible the voices were, as long as the underlying message was reinforced over and over again – that the U.S. and the West is crumbling, corrupt, and hypocritical - intent on destroying Russia and other countries that stand in the way of carrying out its hegemonic goals.

There was a running joke among some employees about adopting this mindset by "drinking the Kool-Aid." I saw how employees and viewers eventually drank it all up. It's the result of being engrossed in an environment where hating America was rewarded. It's a mentality that is perpetuated online by Internet personalities that gain followers and a sense of belonging by spewing hate and disinformation without regard for the truth.

Russian media provides a home for a spectrum of political beliefs as long as they are skeptical of the political establishment. While some of the theories peddled are outright absurd, there are a surprising amount of people prone to being manipulated that think it's hip to believe in any alternative theory, feeling proud of perceiving themselves to be enlightened and even prouder when they amass sizable social media followers that hang on every misguided and outright false theory that is propagated. Russia is aware of this population of paranoid skeptics and plays them like a fiddle.

Those that challenge any narrative against Russia are branded CIA agents, of being puppets for neo-conservatives intent on reigniting a cold war, and face the ire of seemingly countless online trolls or hecklers on the internet that hijack online discussions. I was accused of being all of these things and faced the constant stream of Internet hate for being perceived as such. This is just a minor example of this new propaganda technique in action.

Meanwhile, within Russia, every protest or demonstration, every strained relation with a foreign country, any economic troubles - Russian media would like to convince as much of the world as possible that its woes are the result of Western meddling. The paranoia extends to believing that Western media is not only complicit, but instrumental in ensuring Western dominance.

The Russian bosses say that the organization is simply providing another perspective – one that is ignored by Western media. The implication is that there is no such thing as an objective truth and that every possible theory uttered by anyone is equally plausible. The Kremlin sees this as an opportunity to mold reality.

But let's not get duped by this falsehood. Someone is responsible for pulling the trigger that killed Russian opposition leader Boris Nemtsov. Someone, some entity, is responsible for launching the BUK missile that downed MH17, killing all 298 passengers on board. This is not up for debate or open to interpretation. Because behind the strategically false finger pointing, there is a *true* story. And it both cases, the true story has yet to be uncovered and proven, there are still so many questions that remain unanswered and justice not served for the victims. There is someone that prefers it stays this way.

We shouldn't let it slide. We need to take notice and take action. The best weapon against this rapidly expanding propaganda campaign is the truth. We just need to fight for it. We fight it by refusing to look the other when a lie is told, by not giving undeserved benefit of the doubt after being deceived time and time again, and by spreading awareness about this new disinformation stream that is polluting the airwaves and online discussions which shape our perceptions of world events. We fight it by considering the source, thinking before you click, retweet, or share an article that aims to deceive. While it's true that the truth is oftentimes difficult to uncover and not always immediately apparent, we should seek to find the truth, spread that information, and learn from it - whatever that truth may be.

Chairman ROYCE. Thank you, Ms. Wahl.

Ms. Dale.

STATEMENT OF MS. HELLE C. DALE, SENIOR FELLOW FOR PUBLIC DIPLOMACY, THE HERITAGE FOUNDATION

Ms. DALE. Chairman Royce——

Chairman ROYCE. Helle, could you just hit the button there?

Ms. DALE. Hit the button. I will start again.

Chairman Royce, Ranking Member Engel and distinguished members of the committee, thank you very much for putting together this timely and very important hearing today and for inviting me to speak.

The views I will express are my own and should not be construed as representing the official position of the Heritage Foundation.

I come before you as someone who has studied U.S. public diplomacy for years and as a former journalist. I have interviewed enough dissidents of Cold War days to appreciate the profound importance and the moral obligation we have of reaching citizens of countries under authoritarian or totalitarian control with truthful information.

The recent past has shown that it does make a difference, sometimes changing the course of history itself. Unfortunately, after the end of the Cold War the United States all but disarmed itself in the battle for hearts and minds in Russia and its neighboring countries.

It was assumed that the West had won the ideological battle and strategic decisions were made in public diplomacy and international broadcasting that turned out to be huge mistakes.

Today, we are scrambling to increase broadcasting and digital capacity to counter Russian disinformation. The relevant U.S. agencies in this information war are, of course, primarily the Broadcasting Board of Governors, or the BBG, which oversees all U.S. civilian international broadcasting, the State Department and to some extent the Department of Defense.

To give you a preview of my conclusion, the U.S. Government must ramp up its international broadcasting capacity but it has to be done through the reform of the BBG. At present, this is our most important tool in this information war.

The BBG has over the past decade shut down many language services and radio transmissions which now turn out to be critically important. The motivation has been budget constraints and the desire to focus on the Internet and, at times, satellite television.

In 2008, VOA ended its broadcasts in Russian the very week Russia invaded Georgia. After the invasion, the decision was not reversed.

Short wave radio was abandoned and whatever English language content there was to be rebroadcast in Russia had to be negotiated with Russian local AM and FM stations.

Moscow finally shut down all VOA broadcasting in 2014. But the United States has, as we heard, allowed Russian media to flourish within our own borders in the name of freedom of expression.

RT has impressive television studios right here in the nation's capital. The contrast could not be more stark. The conditions attached to rebroadcasting of VOA English content to Russia were

heavy handed and I just want to give you a short personal anec-
dote.

I was invited on a program, a foreign policy discussion at VOA
in 2012. It was just before the Russian Presidential election and I
asked if we were going to discuss it and I was told no, the management had told them, the journalists, that they could not discuss the
Russian election because Voice of Russia had threatened to cancel
its agreement with the BBG if the U.S. Government allowed VOA
to go ahead with a discussion of the Russian election.

Now, why this mattered so much is hard to understand but a
global audience were thereby deprived of a discussion of the subject.

The management at VOA, the producers, followed orders from
Moscow and it should be mentioned that this is the same manage-
ment that often fiercely resists any editorial influence from the
U.S. Government itself.

Currently, the only content offered from VOA in Russian is Internet-based Skype video and use broadcasts as well as VOA's Russian language Web site. Now, it is argued that the Internet is the
best way to reach Russians because they have a high level of Internet connectivity as an advanced society.

Yet, VOA's Russian service Web site ranks number 3,828 in Russia, which does not compare very well with RT's influence here in
the United States where it is something like number 64.

Radio Free Europe and Radio Liberty, the U.S. Government's
surrogate broadcasters, have run into the same problems as VOA.
They also took a major beating in the international press in 2012
when the management of Radio Liberty fired most of its Moscow
staff.

I can see I am running out of time. I just wanted to mention finally that we are trying to play catch up in reform legislation and
in the BBG's strategy paper produced in 2015. I mean, sorry—for
2015, 2016 on countering a revisionist Russia.

But we are playing catch up here and I would be happy to discuss that further with you.

[The prepared statement of Ms. Dale follows:]

Russia's "Weaponization" of Information

Testimony Presented to the House Foreign Affairs Committee

April 15th, 2015 at 10 am

By Helle C. Dale

My name is Helle Dale. I am Senior Fellow for Public Diplomacy in the Davis Institute for National Security and Foreign Policy at The Heritage Foundation. The views I express in this testimony are my own, and should not be construed as representing any official position of The Heritage Foundation.

Audiences within reach of Russia's growing media empire are increasingly subjected to manipulation and rampant anti-Americanism.[i] This trend has intensified since the Russian annexation of Crimea and its invasion of Eastern Ukraine in 2014. Through its global network, *Russia Today*, (RT) the Kremlin broadcasts globally in five major languages, including on cable stations in the United States. Free Western media has no comparable presence in Russia.

Russian propaganda is corrosive to the image of the United States and to our values. Or as Assistant Secretary of State for Europe Victoria Nuland described it before this committee on March 4th, "the Kremlin's pervasive propaganda campaign, where is truth is no obstacle." And Russian propaganda is being spread aggressively around the world as we have not seen it since Soviet days. This is not just in Central Asia, and Eastern and Central Europe, but even here in the West. The daily content and commentary from RT and others is often polished and slickly-produced. And it's not like old-fashioned propaganda, aimed solely at making Putin and Russia look good. It's a new kind of propaganda, aimed at sowing doubt about anything having to do with the U.S. and the West, and in a number of countries, unsophisticated audiences are eating it up.

The unfortunate fact is that the United States government became complacent in the battle for "hearts and minds" in Russia and its neighboring countries after the end of the Cold War. For Instance, the administration's budget request for 2016 is $751,436 million for U.S. International Broadcasting.[ii] Reportedly, RT has a budget alone of $400 million for its Washington bureau.

Today, the U.S. government is scrambling to increase capacity to counter Russian disinformation. The relevant agencies in this information war are the U.S. government are primarily the Broadcasting Board of Governors (BBG, which oversees all U.S. civilian international broadcasting) and to some extent the State Department and the Department of Defense. The administration has requested for 2016 $693 million for democracy promotion and public diplomacy for Ukraine, Georgia, Moldova and Ukraine to help them withstand pressure from Russia, as Secretary of State John Kerry put it to the HFAC.[iii]

- Let me first describe the position we find ourselves in today.
- Then current efforts by the U.S. government to catch up to the Russians.

- And finally present my recommendations, important among them, the need to reform the BBG.

Where We Are Today

BBG abandons broadcasting to Russia

Motivated by budget constraints and the desire to recalibrate U.S. international broadcasting towards Internet and satellite television, the BBG has over the past decade shut down language services and radio transmissions, which today turn out to be critically important. This has turned out to be a huge strategic mistake.

In 2008, just before the Russian invasion of Georgia. [iv]Following the invasion, which shocked the world, the decision was not reversed, though a 30-minute news broadcast to Russia was salvaged by a persistent BBG member. Remaining were rebroadcasts of English-language programs through highly precarious contracts with Russian FM and AM stations, including the Kremlin's own Voice of Russia.

At present there is no Voice of America broadcasting to Russia, shortwave, AM or FM. Nor are there any television broadcasts to Russia. Shortwave radio was abandoned first after which, AM or FM broadcasts had to be negotiated with Russian local stations. These arrangements came with strings attached. The Russian government finally shut down any VOA broadcasting in 2014.

It has to be recalled that as the Kremlin put the chokehold on U.S. broadcasting, the United States has allowed Russian media to flourish within our own borders in the name of freedom of expression. Russia Today (or RT) has impressive television studios right here in the nation's capital and broadcasts on cable channels throughout the United States.

The conditions attached to Russian rebroadcasting of VOA material were heavy-handed. In one case I personally recall, I had been invited to participate in a VOA foreign policy discussion on an English language program. The program has a global audience and is not aimed specifically at Russian listeners. But it was contracted to be rebroadcast in Russia by Voice of Russia, a state owned service. It was right before the Russian presidential election in March, 2012, and the election would have been an obvious topic for discussion. However, in a particularly shocking example of self-censorship as a consequence of foreign pressure, employees of Voice of America were told by VOA managers to cancel plans for coverage of the Russian presidential election on the day prior to and the day of the Russian vote. The reason? Voice of Russia was threatening to tear up its rebroadcasting agreement with the BBG unless the U.S. government's broadcasters complied with limitations on election coverage imposed by Russian legislation. Russian demands were meekly accepted by the same VOA management that fiercely resists any interference from the U.S. government in the name of editorial independence.

So is there anything left of VOA's Russian presence at a time when Russia is surging in its propaganda war against the United States?

One television news show is broadcast by VOA in Russian into Ukraine. Other than that, currently the only content offered by VOA's Russian service is Internet-based: skype video and news podcasts, as well as VOA's Russian language website. It could be argued that the Internet offers the best outreach to educated Russians, students and opinion-makers. Russia after all enjoys one of the highest levels of Internet penetration of VOA's target audiences. Yet, VOA's Russian service website ranks 3,828 in Russia and 44,415 in the world, according to the Internet service Alexa.[v] (This compares to RT's website, which ranks 61 in Russia 443 in the world, and it should be added 1,007 in the United States.)

Russian propaganda has gone into overdrive in Central and Eastern Europe as well, while Voice of America shut down every language in the region in the early years of the 21st century – Czech, Polish, Croatian, Slovakian, Serbian. The assumption was that the Cold War being over, these were relics of the past and that as members of the EU or aspiring to be that, these countries already have a free press.[vi]

RFE/RL troubles in Russia RL/RFE has run into exactly the same rebroadcasting problems that beset VOA. Radio in FM and AM format has been dependent on contracts with local Russian stations, who are either under the control of the Kremlin or subject to its pressure. Some shortwave radio continues to exist, and RFE/RL continues to broadcast eight hours original content to Russia.

FRE/RL's presence and reputation in Russia, it must be added took a beating in 2012 when new management at FRE/RL's headquarters in Prague decided to fire most of the staff in its Moscow office, some of them veteran journalists who had worked there for decades and were true champions of human rights. The decision came after Russian legislation blocked any AM broadcasting by RFE/RL in Russia, apparently causing a reconsideration of the role of these broadcasters. The result was an international uproar, which eventually cost the RFE/RL director his job. After much bad publicity about the way the U.S. government treats its employees, a report produced for the BBG in March the following year recommended that the staff that had been fired be hired back for their former positions. By then, a lot of damage had unfortunately been done.[vii]

Ukraine

Broadcasting to Ukraine had gone the same way as broadcasting to Russia when fate and Vladimir Putin intervened in March of 2014. As Russia annexed Crimea, started stirring trouble in Eastern Ukraine, and shut down independent media in the areas it controlled, it became clear that the United States (and Europe as well) needed to fashion a response. In the spring and summer of 2014, Radio Liberty/Radio Free Europe put four new programs on the air, aimed at Ukrainian and Russian audiences, though these amount to less than two hours weekly new original content. This is in addition to a daily 5 minute news show. These programs were produced with new congressional funding and are conditioned on continued budgetary commitments.

State Department

On taking office last year, Undersecretary of State for Public Diplomacy and Public Affairs Rick Stengel acknowledged the challenges presented to U.S. public diplomacy by the rise of Russian propaganda as well as the social media campaigns of Middle East terrorist groups like ISIS. He inadvertently made a troubling point. "We need to figure out what to answer when people talk to us," he said. "We have to explain our policy. We should be the nation that listens."

This reflects the Obama administration view of the Internet as the key tool for public diplomacy. It is a view that has caused a de-emphasis of other public diplomacy tools such as U.S. International Broadcasting, one of the largest accounts in the public diplomacy budget, but one that is constantly under stress even as countries such as Russia and China beef up their broadcasting capability.

Stengel acknowledged reliance on the Internet can be problematic. "We are seeing a closing off of the Internet and the information space by illiberal autocracies," he said. "People can close off information space. We did not expect this." He also said he was "amazed at the surge" in Russian propaganda "in the Near Abroad," although growing Internet censorship and other similar Russian behavior have hardly been secrets.[viii]

Today, Russia has a rank of "Partially Free" as regards the Internet and "Not Free" as regards the press, according to "Freedom on the Net 2014," published by Freedom House. [ix]

At present the State department's most successful counter propaganda tool is the Center for Strategic Counterterrorism Communication, whose work is currently aimed at the threat from terrorist groups like ISIS. Yet, the center grew out of the work of State's Digital Response Team, which under President George W. Bush was more broadly based and directed also at propaganda in Europe and the former Soviet Union.

NATO

A potentially promising development is the opening of a new NATO Center of Excellence in Riga, Latvia, a country with a large Russian speaking population. One of the Center's primary tasks will be to counter Russian propaganda, which used to target Latvia's population specifically, but now is a problem throughout Russia's border states and indeed Europe. The Center was only stood up in October, will function as a type of NATO think tank. The United States is still negotiating its contribution, but is expected to conclude an arrangement by June. The Center's new offices will officially open in September.

What Is Being Done?

A new strategy

Having dismantled a lot of the tools for reaching audiences in the post-Soviet space, the BBG has had to be creating about launching a media strategy. This is as difficult as it is critically important. The United States simply cannot walk away the war of ideas, as authoritarian regimes like the Russia (or the Chinese or the Iranian) surge in capacity.

The BBG's "U.S. International Media Strategy Paper FY 2015-16: Countering a Revisionist Russia," dated October 20, 2014, states the necessity to "shape responses that are asymmetric to the Kremlin's tactics," read we don't have the resources to meet the Russian propaganda avalanche head on. Quote:

> *USIM lacks the massive resources that Russia is pouring into its media campaigns at home and abroad, and so must be precisely targeted, efficient, multifaceted and smart; also, because of Kremlin restrictions USIM is not able, with very limited exceptions, to reach audiences in Russia on television (broadcast and cable), by far the most popular sources of news and information." Please note that what used to be U.S. International Broadcasting is now known as USIM (U.S. International Media, reflecting the shift from broadcasting to digital media.*[x]

It took Congressional action to pump life back into the BBG's strategy towards Ukraine. A Congressional appropriation of $10 million for countering Russian propaganda through Voice of America and Radio Liberty/Radio Free Europe. This was good news for Ukrainians. The main goal of this money is to inform mostly Europeans, including those in the states bordering Russia, what is going on in Ukraine. With the elimination of most radio broadcasts to Russia, U.S. broadcasting strategy has shifted to Russia's periphery – and as we have seen to social media.

Following Russia's annexation of Ukraine, and congressional pressure, the BBG created the show "Current Time," a 30-minute news program in Russian, aimed at Russian speakers in the countries along Russia's borders. It is produced by RFE/RL out of Prague, the show is being picked up by stations in Georgia, Lithuania, Moldova, Ukraine, and Latvia.

Interest has been so great from Russia's neighbors that RFE/RL is currently developing a Central Asian version -- with Central Asian hosts and content -- to expand its reach. A new unit at RFE/RL is working to distribute "Current Time" content on social media as well. "Current Time" fights Russian propaganda and the countries are next to Russia are clearly asking for help in pushing back against the disinformation and misinformation coming out of Russia. The BBG's strategy document also includes plans for a North Caucasus version of the show.

Other elements of this strategic plan include ramping up to three to four hours of daily broadcasting by 2016 and in 2017, a 24/7 satellite television channel in Russian, as well as broadcasting aimed at Russian audiences in the United States, something that it now allowed under the revised Smith-Mundt Act.

It goes without saying that such a strategy would also include websites and a YouTube presence, as well as a social media response team. At this stage, that element is unavoidable, but it has to be recalled that Russia's Internet censorship is among the worst in the world

Given the aggressive nature of Russia's current international posture, United States should respond quickly to this demand and ramp up our efforts to fill it. While you cannot fight propaganda with propaganda, nor should the U.S. government sink to the level of sheer disinformation that characterize much Russian propaganda, you can fight it, as Current Time does, by focusing a light on the lies and contrasting them with the facts.

Recommendations:

Reforming the BBG

As a result of the widely perceived decline in the effectiveness of U.S. international broadcasting and of frustrations with the management of the BBG, several attempts have been made to legislate changes to the structure of the enterprise. Numerous independent reports have suggested this course of action, from the Heritage report in 2008, "Reforming U.S. Public Diplomacy for the 21st Century,"[xi] which I co-authored with Tony Blankley, to a brand new report issued by the Woodrow Wilson Center, "Reassessing U.S. International Broadcasting", by Enders Wimbush and Elizabeth Portale.[xii]

Several pieces of legislation have been devoted to broadcasting reform. From the 2009 "Strategic Communications Act – H.R. 489," sponsored by Mac Thornberry to the "U.S. International Communications Reform Act of 2014 -- H.R. 4490," which passed the House of Representatives in July last year. Attempts at reform are invariably met with opposition by the management at the BBG. Yet, considering the challenges the United States is up against, it is imperative that broadcasting is improved. For instance, a newly hired Chief Executive Officer of International Broadcasting, Andrew lack, on whom much hope had been pinned for better management, left the position after only six weeks in the job on March 4th and on April 7th, the Director of Voice of America, David Ensor, announced that he was leaving. The BBG itself, a nine-member part-time board, functions as an executive body, a management anomaly that has been question by many, including the State Department's own Inspector General in a scathing 2013 report.[xiii] To put muscle and focus into U.S. broadcasting strategy, the BBG must be reformed and I hope this hearing will persuade Congress of the urgency of doing so.

Additional recommendations:

- Use public diplomacy to counter anti-American and pro-Russian propaganda by the Russian government. U.S. efforts should include international broadcasting, a new Russian satellite channel, the Internet, social networking, print media, and revamped academic, student, and business exchange programs.
- Respond publicly and vigorously to high-profile Russian falsehoods, while regularly emphasizing the regime's suppression of independent media in Russia.

- Launch a comprehensive audit, led by U.S. intelligence agencies and the State Department's International Information Programs office, of Russian information operations in the United States and its allies, to evaluate the extent and effectiveness of these campaigns and understand their strategic implications.
- Publicize overt and – as compatible with the security of intelligence sources – covert Russian support for Western media outlets to deprive them of credibility.
- Give the same visa treatment to personnel working for Russian state-controlled media that Russia gives to journalists from U.S. and allied nations.
- Recognize that nations such as Georgia, and U.S. allies in Central and Eastern Europe, are particularly vulnerable to Russian propaganda, and focus U.S. support for independent media and journalists on these nations, while, at the strategic level, continuing to back NATO's Strategic Communications Centre of Excellence in Latvia.
- Launch more education programs for Ukrainian journalists particularly those who are involved in covering the situation on the ground in battle zone in Eastern Ukraine. Ninety percent of Ukrainian journalists who cover the conflict don't have any military experience. Many of them lack the necessary equipment like helmets or body armors to work in a battle zone.

The Heritage Foundation is a public policy, research, and educational organization recognized as exempt under section 501(c)(3) of the Internal Revenue Code. It is privately supported and receives no funds from any government at any level, nor does it perform any government or other contract work.

The Heritage Foundation is the most broadly supported think tank in the United States. During 2013, it had nearly 600,000 individual, foundation, and corporate supporters representing every state in the U.S. Its 2013 income came from the following sources:

Individuals 80%

Foundations 17%

Corporations 3%

The top five corporate givers provided The Heritage Foundation with 2% of its 2013 income. The Heritage Foundation's books are audited annually by the national accounting firm of McGladrey, LLP.

Endnotes:

[1] Daniel Kochis, "Countering Russian Propaganda Abroad," Heritage Foundation *Issue Brief* No. 4286, October 21, 2014, http://www.heritage.org/research/reports/2014/10/countering-russian-propaganda-abroad.

[ii] United States Advisory Commission on Public Diplomacy, "2014 Comprehensive Annual Report on Public Diplomacy and International Broadcasting," U.S. Department of State, December 11, 2014. http://www.state.gov/pdcommission/reports/235008.htm

[iii] Russia Insider: "John Kerry Seeks Congress Funds to Counter RT," February 26, 2015. http://russia-insider.com/en/politics_opinion/2015/02/26/3898

[iv] Helle C. Dale et al., "Challenging America: How Russia, China, and Other Countries Use Public Diplomacy to Compete with the U.S.," Heritage Foundation *Backgrounder* No. 2698, June 21, 2012, http://www.heritage.org/research/reports/2012/06/challenging-america-how-russia-china-and-other-countries-use-public-diplomacy-to-compete-with-the-us

[v] Alexa. Golos-ameriki.ru. http://www.alexa.com/siteinfo/golos-ameriki.ru

[vi] Ariel Cohen, PhD, and Helle C. Dale, "Russian Anti-Americanism: A Priority Target for U.S. Public Diplomacy," Heritage Foundation *Backgrounder* No. 2373, February 24, 2010, http://www.heritage.org/research/reports/2010/02/russian-anti-americanism-a-priority-target-for-us-public-diplomacy

[vii] Ariel Cohen PhD, and Helle C. Dale, "How to Save Radio Liberty," Heritage Issue brief #3804, December 13, 2012. http://www.heritage.org/research/reports/2012/12/how-to-save-radio-liberty

[viii] Helle C. Dale, "What Should Be U.S. Diplomacy Strategy in a Time of Terrorism?" The Daily Signal, September 19, 2014. http://dailysignal.com/2014/09/19/u-s-diplomacy-strategy-time-terrorism/

[ix] Freedom House, "Freedom on the Net 2014." Washington, New York, December, 2014. https://freedomhouse.org/report/freedom-net/freedom-net-2014#.VSrdybBFCUl

[x] Broadcasting Board of Governors, "U.S. International Media Strategy Paper FY 2015-16: Countering a Revisionist Russia," October 20, 2014.

[xi] Tony Blankley, Helle C. Dale and Oliver Horn, "Reforming U.S. Public Diplomacy for the 21st century," Heritage Foundation Backgrounder No. 2211, November 20th, 2008, http://www.heritage.org/research/reports/2008/11/reforming-us-public-diplomacy-for-the-21st-century.

[xii] Enders Wimbush, Elizabeth Protale, "Rethinking U.S. International Broadcasting," Woodrow Wilson Center, Washington, April 22, 2015. http://www.wilsoncenter.org/event/rethinking-us-international-broadcasting-conversation-mission-strategy-and-organization

---

[xiii] U.S. Department of State and the Broadcasting Board of Governors, Office of Inspector General, "Inspection of the Broadcasting Board of Governors," January 2013, p. 1, http://oig.state.gov/documents/organization/203193.pdf

Chairman ROYCE. Thank you. Thank you, Ms. Dale.

One of the questions I am interested in here is that usually around the globe people hunger for information and especially when they think they are being denied facts.

But what seems to be happening in Russia is that people begin to presume that these conspiracies are in fact true as they are, you know, introduced to this on a daily basis.

They repeat it over and over and over again and suddenly the conspiratorial theories begin to take on a life of its own, and I wondered if maybe the panelists could explain the factors that make this Russian disinformation campaign seemingly so effective from some of the polling I have seen inside Russia in terms of the credibility the people have to information which logic would contradict. But also I was going to ask you a little bit about the platform that it provides for fringe and radical views, not just in Russia but worldwide, as sort of the extreme fringe as given a platform for what otherwise would not be considered reputable television, you know. Most broadcasts wouldn't have on the types of voices with these conspiratorial theories.

But maybe you could explain the process that RT undertakes to select its experts, and I will just turn it over to the panel for your responses.

Ms. WAHL. That is an interesting question, selecting the experts, because that word, I think, is used loosely in Russian television. Essentially, anybody that is an expert is somebody that is willing to toe the Russian line and to—I mean, they could be from the far left, they could be from the far right, they could have unconventional deranged theories.

It didn't matter, and sometimes the producers would scour the Internet for these experts. So what qualifies as an expert it is kind of murky what that is.

And why it is effective, I think you had mentioned that it provides this voice for fringe voices, extremists and it works because it provides a place for these people, a place where these people can congregate and feed off of each other's biases.

It is almost like a community that is almost like a cult, I would say, that is formed online and they mobilize and they feel like they are part of some enlightened fight against the establishment and they find a home.

They find a place where they are heard and they find a sense of belonging. They find an outlet where they can—where they can— a platform to voice their deranged views.

And I know that formally of Radio Free Europe Mr. Lack, who has since departed, had gotten a lot of criticism for comparing Russia today and Russian propaganda to ISIS propaganda.

And while yes, there is a strong difference—we are talking about a terrorist organization versus a government—you know, a nation state, I think he did have credence and in comparing the strategy that is there by using the Internet to mobilize people that feel displaced, that feel like they have been on the outskirts of society and give them a place where they can find a sense of belonging and maybe make a difference in their own way, and it is a problem and we see that it is effective.

We see that they are shaping the discussion online, on message boards, on Twitter, on social media. And the Internet—you know, we thought that it would be this place where, you know, it is wonderful in a lot of ways because a lot of different viewpoints and a lot of different people have a voice like never before.

But, unfortunately, it has provided a forum where disinformation, false theories, people that are just trying to make a name for themselves, bloggers or whatever, that have absolutely no accountability for the truth are able to rile up a massive amount of people online for——

Chairman ROYCE. Well, I think what is interesting about it—I mean, the use of raw violence, which they do a lot of on YouTube, 1.4 billion hits is a lot of hits.

Ms. WAHL. Yes.

Chairman ROYCE. So people will go to the use of raw violence and then that will be used as, you know, part of a thesis on some conspiracy theory that then is played out. I wondered, Peter, your take on this.

Mr. POMERANTSEV. This question—you have hit on one of the key issues here, which goes—takes us all the way through the problems at stake. They are not fringe anymore, these groups. We are talking about a France where Jean Marie Le Pen's far right party is surging in the polls.

We are talking about a Hungary where Jobbik, the far right party, is rising, rising. We are talking about 20 percent of parliamentarians in the European Parliament having what we used to think were fringe, very pro-Russian views.

Among the people who vote for these parties there is a lot of people who believe in conspiracies because they are working on a similar thing.

Conspiracies happen when people don't trust the institutions around them, don't trust Parliament, don't trust media. Everyone is lying to you? Then there must be a shadowy hand. So the Kremlin is in this loop.

It is pushing out more conspiracies to fan that audience. They are funding these parties. You know, we know that the Kremlin is funding Jean Marie Le Pen in France. These are not fringe parties. This is actually now becoming the mainstream and this is very, very frightening. Conspiracy is—what is conspiracy? Sort of a linguistic sabotage on the infrastructure of reason.

You know, you can't have a reality-based discussion when everything becomes conspiracy. In Russia, the whole discourse is conspiracy. Everything is conspiracy. When a genuine opposition person like Alexander Navalny emerged in Russia, the first thing the Kremlin does?

He is one of ours—he is a conspiracy as well. Don't believe in him. Sort of about destroying belief in anything. When you have no believe in truth then you can't believe in anything.

But also more insidiously than that, look, our—I am going to get very grand now—our global order is based on the idea of reality-based politics.

If that reality-based sort of, you know, base is destroyed then you can't have, you know, international institutions and international dialogue. I mean, I remember a quote from, I think, a Franciscan monk after the Second World War.

He is, like, lying is not a form of communication. It rids people of their right to live in reality and makes reality-based politics impossible. This is a very insidious trend.

Chairman ROYCE. Thank you, Peter. Let me go. My time has expired. I am going to go to Mr. Engel of New York.

Mr. ENGEL. Thank you, Mr. Chairman.

Let me start with you, Mr. Pomerantsev. Some of the distortions coming out of the Kremlin are just absurd. For instance, blaming Ukraine or the United States for the shooting down of that Malaysian Airlines flight over Ukraine.

But as three of you have mentioned, we know these messages are taking hold. Can you give us a bit more detail about the major messages being driven by Moscow and describe how those messages are affecting public opinion among Russian speakers in the frontline countries?

And could you also tell us what your sense is of the way our other European allies are looking at the problem? Do you they not see the problem—our Western allies?

What steps have other governments taken to respond to Russian propaganda and is it having any great effect?

Mr. POMERANTSEV. That is a lot of questions. So, listen, I just read a very interesting study of Estonia where actually got into the weeds of who believes what, right.

So there is a certain amount of the population who just watch Russian TV and they buy the Russian lie. The message has been changing. First, it was a fascist revolution. Then it was a NATO conspiracy.

Now it is the Ukrainians who are the fascists. It is always changed and changing. It is not about establishing a truth. It is about coming up with crazier and crazier stories, which are meant to be emotionally engaging.

The Russian deputy minister for communication openly says that truth in journalism doesn't matter. It is all about, you know, coming up with fantasies that are powerful.

So the message changes but, you know, it is clear. It is the West's fault. Ukraine is a zone of chaos. Russia is a zone of stability. That is a very big one. You know, like, Russia equals stability, Ukraine equals chaos.

Everywhere that America goes equals chaos and so on and so forth. So there is some interlocking narratives but they shift. But what is interesting in Estonia—so there is a small percentage of people who just watch that and believe in it.

A bigger one and a more active one, the younger people, watch both Estonian and Russian. But they don't just end up not believing in anything.

They just end up completely confused and completely passive and so this really challenges some old ideas that if we could just get the truth out there like in the Cold War we will win. It is a much more intricate challenge nowadays.

We have to not only get the truth out there, we have to win trust, which might mean a much cleverer and deeper and actually sort of more thoughtful form of programming to make.

As for European countries, it is a real mix. The frontline countries are, obviously, very alarmed because for them it is an existential threat. Britain is aware. Germany is aware.

I think as you go further and further they care less and less, and some countries are far more interested in their financial relationships with Moscow and don't perceive Eastern Europe maybe as their problem. But hopefully that is shifting.

Mr. ENGEL. Ms. Wahl, you—as you mentioned in your testimony you have seen Russian propaganda up close. You left Russia Today because you refused to be a mouthpiece for the Kremlin and since then you yourself have been a target.

You mentioned propaganda. Since that time we have seen Russia Today open up shop in more places round the world. Can you give us some detail about the strategy behind the growth of Russia Today around the world and the specific methods used by Russia Today so-called journalists to advance Moscow's message?

Ms. WAHL. Right, yes. It is true that since my resignation that Russian media has only grown. There was a channel that was opened up in London and Berlin.

There was a video organization called Ruptly that was formed. Sputnik also launched—it is also funded by the Russian Government as in dozens of—dozens of cities throughout the world.

That is rapidly expanding, and we are seeing a lot of—a lot more resources being devoted to Russian propaganda. Meanwhile, as we had mentioned earlier, before independent voices has been—have been shut down and, well, what is behind it?

Mr. Pomerantsev touched on it before. It is that just putting this narrative out there that the West is really the evil hypocritical corrupt player here and that for far too long the West has been dominating the conversation and they are inserting themselves now as an alternative, as somebody that is telling the other part of the story.

But I saw that that, indeed, was not the case, that this was actually manipulation. And I guess another thing about conspiracy theories it seems like a bizarre thing. I mean, who believes in these bizarre conspiracy theories?

And I think what is interesting is that it doesn't really matter. You don't need to believe the conspiracy theory as a whole to be confused as to what is really going on. I am going to use my experience as an example.

The narrative that RT put out about me and kind of their friends was that I was simply just a puppet intent on reigniting the Cold War—that, basically, that I had had no mind of my own and strings were being pulled and that the intent there is that it was some nefarious intent to reignite a cold war.

Now, a lot of people hear that and it seems farfetched and it is not true. But if you—by just putting that narrative out there and by the trolls retweeting it and repeating it so often, it becomes a thing.

It becomes part of the discussion. It becomes part of the discourse, and after a while you have to address it because it is out there. The seeds of doubt have already been planted and first impressions matter.

And even if you don't believe that I was a puppet in that way, it still shaped the narrative in terms of casting doubt on my credibility, on my motivations, on what really went on.

So that is kind of just a small example of how conspiracy theory works. You know, you don't have to necessarily believe that 9/11 was an inside job completely but if you have that out there in so many other nefarious plots a viewer gets kind of confused and thinks maybe the truth is somewhere in the middle.

Maybe it wasn't orchestrated but surely the West was instrumental in letting it happen in one way or another. So I think that is one way that conspiracy theories work is that it just causes chaos and confusion and even people that are seemingly logical and not prone to this type of manipulation are—I see that they are affected by it because if you see the constant stream of chatter online it does kind of start to get to you.

And I saw that there, especially within RT where you are constantly exposed to these articles and this anti-American, anti-Western rhetoric.

You are kind of in this vacuum where you kind of think whoa, you know, maybe Russia has a point. Maybe there is some truth there that is to be uncovered.

And so I think it is important to kind of come to terms, and it is bizarre and it is kind of strange to grasp but these strange conspiracy theories that are put out there really are aimed at just disrupting and deceiving and causing chaos so nobody really knows what the truth is.

Chairman ROYCE. We will go now to Dana Rohrabacher of California.

Mr. ROHRABACHER. Well, having been a former journalist myself and know about the way our journalist profession works in the United States, and I have been very interested in your analysis that truth is the way that we should fight this threat and I agree with that.

I would hope that we are honest enough with one another to realize that we have major flaws in our dissemination of facts and information in the United States as well.

So the truth may well be what we have heard today in the testimony, that Russia is engaged in a major effort to basically support its own policies and promote changes and effects on other populations that further the interests of Russia.

I would be surprised if that wasn't the case. Let me just note that so I can accept everything that was said here I would have preferred, Mr. Chairman, that we had at least one other person to balance out this in a way that perhaps could have compared our system to the Russian system and to find out where that truth is, just how bad that is.

There are, by the way, I am convinced there are people here in the United States who want us to have the same status toward Russia today as we had during the Cold War and they still believe that this—we should be in a Cold War status and that Russia is today the same as it was under communism and that Putin is Brezhnev, if not Hitler.

And I don't believe that necessarily those people who are pro-
moting that concept are any more accurate than the Russians that
you are now talking about presenting their concepts.

You know, I—frankly, I think there is a little bit of fanaticism
on both sides that don't hear both sides and if we are going to have
peace in this world we have got to be disciplined ourselves in
searching for that truth.

And I just say that when I was a newsman I remember covering
stories and I don't want to be too—I won't name the exact publications but I know major publications that would not cover a story
that made us Republicans look good and all the journalists who
worked for some very strong newspapers in southern California
were just basically propaganda for the liberal left position in our
political spectrum.

And I saw that and, yeah, so we have bias here and they have
bias there and let us find out what the truth is and I would have
preferred, as I say, Mr. Chairman, would have had at least someone to talk about that, to give us that type of analysis.

But I am very happy that we have this information being presented to us today. Let me just ask this about, you know, the stories. What caused you to leave RT? RT is, obviously, a Russian
propaganda outlet. I mean, obviously, it is.

I mean, we would expect it to be, and we have private—that is
why we have private media in the United States so we don't have
our Government setting a policy for what the information will flow.

But I will have to say that in terms of this whole conflict in
Ukraine, when I—almost everybody I know no one ever starts the
scenario about what was going on in Ukraine with the violent over-
throw of an elected President. They always started with the scenario where Russian troops came in.

I happen to oppose any idea that Russian troops should ever
have been introduced in that country but I also recognize that a
democratically-elected President was violently overthrown in order
to achieve certain political objectives in that country.

And so I would hope that we search for the truth and that we
understand that all of the horrible things that you are talking
about today and the direction of the Russian Government out to
get—make sure its interests are being taken care of by propaganda
offensive, we understand that.

But that we have the discipline to be honest and seek the truth
ourselves and not just fall into this Hitler—Putin is Hitler and this
is—and Russia hasn't changed since the Cold War.

We don't need another Cold War. We don't need to be—to take
such belligerent stands and I will tell you I find that belligerence
on both sides of this fight.

Ms. WAHL. I absolutely—can I respond to that?

Mr. ROHRABACHER. Sure.

Ms. WAHL. Okay, and I absolutely hear what you are saying. I
mean, I certainly don't want another Cold War. I think—I can't—
I bet you most people in this room don't want another Cold War,
and I hear what you are saying there, that there is—and I think
what it—I am not arguing that our media here is perfect.

But I think what I am going to have to push back on with your
statements is that in a way that kind of rhetoric kind of equates

our media here—Western media—with what is happening in authoritarian governments like Russia.

It is providing this false equivalence that simply just does not—they do not go hand in hand. There is—there is essential differences, and Russia, yes, they look at our media within the U.S. and they see it in disrepair.

They see, you know, Fox News is known as being conservative. MSNBC is known as being liberal, and therefore everything is a matter of perspective. But there is a difference. There is a difference in that I think it goes to intent.

I think that instead of it being maybe a Republican viewpoint or a liberal viewpoint, what have you, whatever, that there is an intent to actual—to actually advocate and manipulate a war for an authoritarian leader's foreign policy objectives and actually fabricating facts, twisting truths, making up lies. And I understand that, yes, the media is not perfect.

But to compare the two and to say that they are morally or ethically equivalent in any way I think is actually giving some strength to Putin and this propaganda machine and I think he manipulates that mind set and the ability for us here in the United States to be critical of our own media and that is another essential difference because here we can be.

Here, we can call out—I mean, look at Brian Williams. He makes a little flub, he is gone. He is assassinated on Twitter.

Mr. ROHRABACHER. Truth—your point is taken.

Ms. WAHL. It is just not—and I do understand what you are saying and I am not here to make excuses for our own media or say that it is perfect.

But I think that by saying or making any kind of moral equivalence that we are giving power to Russian media and the growing machine. So I think we just have to be cautious in that regard.

Chairman ROYCE. We will go now to Mr. Gregory Meeks.

Mr. MEEKS. Thank you, Mr. Chairman, and thank you, Ms. Wahl, for your push back.

I just, on this subject, will say that I think you are right in the sense that I wouldn't have any problem with RT if there were other media outlets in Russia, you know, various perspectives and that is what, you know, I think is tremendously different in the United States.

You know, we have—you know, I listen to Fox, as you said, and I think that is propaganda and the other side listens to MSNBC. But at least you have two or three and you have other alternatives of which you can listen to so that you can then make your determination as to where and what is—you know, where you are for.

Whereas, from where I am understanding, there is no government-ran institution. RT seems to be financed exclusively by the government which means that they can exclude anything that does not favor the government.

We would have a tremendous problem here if in fact, for example, you know, what we have dialogue right now, whatever side, whoever is the President of the United States. If Barack Obama was able to just put out his side without anything else, you know, we would be up in arms in this country.

I know when George Bush was President if the paper just only put out George Bush's side I would have had a big problem. The fact of the matter is you can have the argument on both sides.

You can't go after the press and, you know, and I don't like some of the things that the press writes but they have the right to write it based upon our Constitution and I think that is a major difference.

So for me, as opposed to focusing on because they, Russia, and how they run is different than what we do in the United States and I understand that CNN, for example, international can play inside of Russia but it is not in the Russian language so it is only in English so therefore people don't understand that.

So my then concern will then go to what takes place outside of Russia, I think, is where Mr. Engel was going as far as the influence so that other areas can have equitable opportunity to listen to all sides.

Russian TV is there, can we—do we have other, whether it is local television from, you know, maybe in Moldova or in Georgia where they are countering or have more freedom to say what the other side is.

Do we have America—what can we do to make sure that that choice that I am talking about that we have in America, particularly within the European countries, that we have—that they have the choice and are not listening to one thing but multiple things.

And I am not saying cut out Russia or RT. I am saying make sure they have all of the evidence so that they can then make a determination of what they believe or don't believe as we do here.

Mr. POMERANTSEV. Well, I will take it first if that is okay.

I mean, I think—I think actually once upon a time we actually intuited the right idea when—you know, when the BBG had Radio Liberty, had Radio Svoboda—the Russian branch of RFE.

The concept worked there, which is the right concept, as surrogate news. Not us believing in the truth. That is always—you know, if you've got "America is evil" in their heads you are not going to believe anything.

Mr. MEEKS. That is correct.

Mr. POMERANTSEV. There is going to be wall there. So it is about going to local issues, finding local voices, local access and it is not just about truth.

I really is about developing a different level of what journalism is. It is almost like the methodology because there is—look, Ukraine, Moldova, you have got oligarch channels, you have gone—you know, it is like one—do you think Fox News is a bit—is a bit sort of, you know, slangy and truthiness? There it is crazy.

You know, like that is—what they lack is not another opinion. There is a lot of bullhorns there. What they lack is that central pillar of education and understanding of how you, you know, think rationally, critically, what evidence is.

So it is both education and this kind of tradition that Radio Svoboda represents and it still represents—it is just so underfunded—of finding local voices who, you know, spread that culture. So I think that is the secret. It is going local and much deeper.

Ms. DALE. May I make a remark? I think you are absolutely right that the diversity of views and the diversity of news is what we thrive on in this country and we are fortunate that we can make up—listen to whatever we want and make up our own mind about what we think is the truth and oftentimes a lot of people reporting from different perspectives will arrive at something that looks like the facts.

Well, in Russia and in the countries—areas that they occupy like eastern Ukraine they were shut down, the independent media—any media that is not controlled by them the moment that they move in and that is how you persuade a local population of one point of view.

It permeates the airwaves to a degree we don't see here at all and can't probably comprehend and I hear this from Ukrainians on the ground.

The moment the Russians come into a town you will start to hear different points of views from their friends and family who live there because suddenly they have been presented with a set of facts which are only from one perspective and that is the one of the Russian Government.

I want to commend Peter for saying that the journalists and raising the level of journalism is important. We can support journalists.

As far as journalistic outlets—trained journalists—in Ukraine the journalists who work in the battle zone don't even—many of them don't have any body armor. They don't have any helmets.

They don't—they are not equipped in any way, shape or form for reporting from front lines and yet they are trying. We here in the United States have the means to support them materially and with training and that, I think, would be—establishing some credibility and some credible voices that trust in the journalistic enterprise that is missing as something that we need to work on to interject in Russia, Ukraine and the countries that are under its influence. Mr. POMERANTSEV. Just to be clear, we were talking about different bits of Ukraine so my colleague is talking about the Ukraine bit that is occupied by the Russians. I was talking about the rest of it, which is pretty chaotic as well in other ways.

Chairman ROYCE. We go to Mr. Scott Perry of Pennsylvania.

Mr. PERRY. Thank you, Mr. Chairman. I apologize for not being here up front.

I was next door at another committee hearing, and I hope to get to some questions but I think it is important for the record to give some people a sense of history they might not know because we have people in this country and around the world that are apologists for what Russia and other similar nations and viewpoints are doing and so I think it is important to reflect on the past and know that this has been going on—this is nothing new.

And so I am just going to read—this is out of a book published in 1986, I think, called "The Harvest of Sorrow" and it is in regard to the terror famine forced on Ukraine by the USSR and Russia.

So the first passage is—that I will read,

"And even more striking or at least a more important aspect of the psychopathy of Stalinism may be seen in the fact that no word about the famine was allowed to appear in the press or elsewhere. People who referred to it were subject to arrest for anti-Soviet propaganda, usually getting 5 or more years in labor camps."

And then,

> "Hitler approvingly calls the big lie. He knew that even when the truth may be readily available, the deceiver need not give up.
> "He saw that the flat denial on one hand and the injection into the pool of information of the corpus of positive falsehood on the other were sufficient to confuse the issue for the passively uninstructed foreign audience and to induce acceptance of the Stalinist version of those actively seeking to be deceived,"

and I have got a few more here that I found interesting.

> This is in regard to a gentleman named Walter Duranty who reported or failed to report or misreported on the famine of the time who was working for the New York Times. This passage says that

> "What the American public got was not the straight stuff but the false reporting. Its influence was enormous and long-lasting."

Furthermore, regarding Duranty, who was a Pulitzer Prize winner for the New York Times based on his work in Ukraine, the praise which went to Duranty was, clearly, not due to a desire to know the truth but, rather, a desire—to a desire of many to be told what they wished to hear and, of course, his own motives needed no explaining.

One communist gave as the reason or one of the reasons for the suppression of the truth the fact that the USSR could not only win the support of workers in the capitalist countries if the human cost of its policies was concealed.

So I do have a little time for some questions and that is just part of the historical perspective of what has been refined over time, and Americans and free people around the globe must be—must be apprised of this and must be aware of it and must be prepared to fight for their freedoms because if they don't will fall prey to the same thing.

I am going to just say Peter, if that is okay with you, the question I think I have for you and I apologize if it has already been asked, there are reports of think tanks becoming puppets of Putin, and I think you have identified the Institute for Democracy and Cooperation in New York as one in particular, if that is true.

What is the strategy behind co-opting these think tanks? Is the strategy working?

Mr. POMERANTSEV. I think—I think that is—I haven't researched that place myself but I think that is quite openly—from as far as I know and can recall right now is quite openly an extension of the Kremlin. I think they do stuff like publishing America's human rights problems.

As Mr. Rohrabacher said, you know, we all have faults so let us just play that game. Much more troubling in many ways is that because there was such—a little bit of a collapse in the funding of Russia studies after the Cold War—there is a famous New Yorker cartoon with a homeless man standing on Fifth Avenue with a little—you know, a little board saying "Give money. I am a Russia expert"—so there was a collapse in funding and the Russians kind of stepped into that breach.

So a lot of intellectuals were kind of drawn toward that. There is the Valdai Forum, which is a very, very clever little operation where, you know, the world's Russia experts get treated like royalty to get to meet Putin once a year and that is sort of like subtly—they know they are being spun but they are still being spun.

There is a game going on there. So it is really about us. We collapsed our funding for Russia studies and, you know, the Kremlin could step in. It is very important to have. The Kremlin understands the values of intellectuals. Stalin understood it.

Lenin understood it. They understand the virtue of having these sort of higher up people. More obviously is their recruitment of former statesman Gerhard Schroder, who works for Gazprom, who has become, you know, Putin's spokesman in Germany in many ways.

In Britain, we have the phenomenon of the Lords on the boards, so various peers who, on the one hand, politically they are just in the House of Lords. On the other hand, you know, they are all working for Russian companies, and they are against sanctions against Russia.

So co-opting elites—intellectual elites, sort of public figures, is very much part of their plan and I think it is actually sometimes more dangerous than RT because RT is kind of out there. We see it.

You know, it's like, whoa. This is stuff happening that where we don't quite see it and in a way far more—far more disturbing.

So to pick up on one thing that you said, that it is not new, disinformation is as old as "The Iliad" and the Trojan Horse—greatest disinformation operation ever. But there is new things going on.

Firstly, the intensity—the information age. The intensity of technology makes the power of technology so much more pervasive and can do so much more with it. We have created this beast called the Internet. We are only just understanding how powerful it can be. So that really changes the intensity of propaganda that you can do.

Also, look, there—I mean, you weren't here at the start. I tried to explain a bit of Russia's idea of information and psychological war.

They see this as the war of the 21st century, a war where you kind of defeat another side in the realms of perception, economy, culture without ever actually invading them—just by breaking a country without ever—without ever having sent troops across.

I gave the example of Estonia. That is different. That is a new idea of war. Usually, you know, the Clauswitzian idea of war is, like, you know, war is a continuation of politics. Politics ends, you have a war, you go back to peace.

This is permanent war, you know, and information and psychological war is permanent, it is endless subversion, endless destabilization. It is a complete rejection of the idea of globalization as a win-win rules-based system where we all agree to profit from each other and it is an idea that integration is actually a way to mess with the other side endlessly.

So we always ask what does Putin want. He sees the 21st century that is going to be like this—endless subversion, disinformation, economic manipulation—and he might be right. I mean, there is a great study of the Chinese three-way warfare in Asia where they are doing something very similar using legal, media and psychological warfare to bully the Philippines and other neighboring states.

They don't do it toward us. You know, they wouldn't. They just do it toward people they've had. ISIS has come up several times. The age of information is becoming the age of disinformation and sort of in the 21st century wars might be decided by whose story line wins, not what happens on the ground.

It might not even matter anymore that NATO has the biggest troops. All that the Russians have to do is make NATO look ridiculous by subverting Article 5 and then the whole narrative edifice comes crumbling down.

So there is something new going on. We are all trying to work out what it is. But I look at other people studying this and I can see we are all coming to similar conclusions.

Mr. PERRY. Thank you, Mr. Chairman. I yield.

Chairman ROYCE. We go now to Joaquin Castro of Texas.

Mr. CASTRO. Thank you, Chairman, and thank you to each of the witnesses for your testimony and for your scholarship and your experiences on these issues.

Mr. Pomerantsev, you mentioned the development of conspiracy theories and particularly on the far right in Russia the development of those conspiracy theories.

I would ask you, do you see that spreading anywhere else? Is Russia the worst actor with respect to this or how do you see that developing in other nations?

Mr. POMERANTSEV. No, sir. Maybe I was unclear. No, no. It is spreading within the far right, which is now mainstream in Europe, in France, Hungary——

Mr. CASTRO. So you are speaking of Europe generally?

Mr. POMERANTSEV. In France——

Mr. CASTRO. Sure.

Mr. POMERANTSEV [continuing]. Hungary, Slovakia. Those are the countries that have been studied and these parties are becoming mainstream. The people who support them are into conspiracy theories because, you know, they are into the far right——

Mr. CASTRO. Sure.

Mr. POMERANTSEV [continuing]. Because they don't trust media government so they are drawn toward conspiracy theories.

Mr. CASTRO. Well, and I guess let me point out my colleague, Mr. Rohrabacher, mentioned—you know, made reference to liberalism in the United States.

But we have a few Presidential candidates running for President of the United States who have also cozied up to people who are conspiracy theorists and who themselves espouse conspiracy theories. Could you speak on that?

Mr. POMERANTSEV. I just don't know the details of that. But this is a global problem. I mean, globalization generally has led to a breakdown of trust. We can't tell is our Government in charge. You know, everybody feels insecure.

A butterfly flaps its wings in China and a town in Michigan goes bust. So we all feel insecure. We all feel that those old bonds of trust are creaking a little bit and conspiracy theories are the result.

That is what I mean. The Kremlin can see what is going on in Europe and the world. That is why it plays on conspiracy theories. They are not being stupid. They can see this is rising everywhere and they are trying to feed it.

In Europe they even fund the—you know, it is a cycle. They feed the conspiracy theories and then fund the parties who represent that constituency.

You know, you have got a nice little thing going on. You know, this is—this is—the Kremlin thinks it is on the right interpretation of history.

They think this is the way the 21st century is going to be—chaotic with no idea of stable reality, no stable global institutions and in that context the country or the state or even the non-state actor who can be the most subversive, who can lie best and be the most kind of, you know, the most subversive—there is no better word, sorry—that state will win.

It is a rejection of 21st century based on kind of rules and institutions. They are saying don't believe anyone—don't believe your institutions—just follow the, you know——

Mr. CASTRO. Well, and I guess my question is, and if any of you would like to comment on it, do you see—I mean, should we be worried about that in the United States or the Americas? Is it something that is particular to Russia and to Europe?

Ms. WAHL. I think that it is something that we should be worried about here because I think that that is kind of the aim of where I saw at Russia Today at the U.S. bureau is that they are trying to mobilize this group of people that are anti-Western, prone to conspiracy theories, people that are so skeptical and paranoid about the establishment, that are disillusioned, that think that the mainstream media is not only complicit but instrumental in carrying out Western dominance.

There is a population of people within the U.S. that believe in this. And yes, they are a fringe, but as Mr. Pomerantsev had pointed out, they are coming out and they are branding together and they are finding a place on the Internet to come together and to make an impact and to make an effect.

And I saw while I was there there was a strong focus on former— I am sure you are well aware of him, former Congressman Ron Paul, and he was kind of the celebrated voice, the celebrated candidate— Presidential candidate.

Why? Well, I mean, I am not going to make an analysis of, you know, his policies and, well, how I personally feel toward them.

But he was seen as kind of like the rock star candidate, the alternative, somebody that is against, you know, intervention, that is very open to speaking out against Western meddling, Western hegemony.

So they do kind of cling to these kinds of voices that tend to be favorable to Russian foreign policy. I am not sure that it is quite equivalent to what we are seeing in Hungary and elsewhere or in the Baltic countries where there is large populations of Russian speakers and ethnic Russians that might be more susceptible.

But yes, they are trying to find this group within the West and even within here in the United States and trying to mobilize them in any way possible, and the thing about these people is that they are loud on the Internet.

They comment on forums. They tweet. They share articles. They are—they do. They make an impact. They shape the discussion——

Mr. CASTRO. Sure.

Ms. WAHL [continuing]. Whether we like it or not, and I do want to comment on, Congressman, earlier about how this is nothing new, and I mentioned earlier that yeah, Russia does have a history of propaganda.

But we are seeing something new here and I think that from my experience what I have come to realize is that the Kremlin is being savvy by using Western media as a model by kind of, you know, making it look sexy with slick graphics and kind of trying to use the Western model.

And it is not propaganda all the time. There are some valid stories on there. But you kind of sneak in the disinformation among the facts and especially when it comes to a war, Ukraine, is where this organization was able to be mobilized and actually used as a tool for—to further war interests.

So yes, it is having an impact within the U.S., in my opinion and from what I have seen.

Ms. DALE. If I could just make a remark on what we could and should be doing from our side, because it is very easy to kind of feel like the Internet takes over your brain and suddenly, you know, you feel like your head is going to explode.

I think it is critically important that part of our strategy is to, within the U.S. Government and within the news organizations that are independent, to try to expose what is going on so that when you do see a credible news organization suddenly being sponsored by the Russian Government or advertising supplements in the newspapers or things that happen online that we have a response team, preferably interagency within the U.S. Government or within possibly collaborating with other organizations that we do not just sit in a receptive mode but that—as we did during the Cold War.

Yes, this is a different age but I think the principles that applied then still apply today, that an untruth has to be confronted by a truth. That is really the only thing you can fight it with.

You may—the volume may be different today but the principle has to be the same and we had that capacity in the past. In the past, we fought Soviet disinformation very effectively and eventually saw the end of the Soviet Union.

I am confident that today, if we put together a sufficient strategy, we can do the same thing and we should.

Chairman ROYCE. Let me just thank Mr. Peter Pomerantsev and Ms. Dale, Elizabeth Wahl. Thank you very, very much for your testimony today.

I also wanted to thank the reporters here who report in Moldova and in Belarus, Ukraine, Georgia, Russia, for being with us and these reporters in particular have been targeted by the Kremlin.

So we wanted to give them an opportunity to be with us today. We are going to have to stand adjourned at this time but we will continue this dialogue.

And thank you to all our panelists.

[Whereupon, at 11:28 a.m., the committee was adjourned.]

APPENDIX

<small>MATERIAL SUBMITTED FOR THE RECORD</small>

FULL COMMITTEE HEARING NOTICE
COMMITTEE ON FOREIGN AFFAIRS
U.S. HOUSE OF REPRESENTATIVES
WASHINGTON, DC 20515-6128

Edward R. Royce (R-CA), Chairman

April 15, 2015

TO: MEMBERS OF THE COMMITTEE ON FOREIGN AFFAIRS

You are respectfully requested to attend an OPEN hearing of the Committee on Foreign Affairs, to be held in Room 2172 of the Rayburn House Office Building (and available live on the Committee website at http://www.ForeignAffairs.house.gov):

DATE: Wednesday, April 15, 2015

TIME: 10:00 a.m.

SUBJECT: Confronting Russia's Weaponization of Information

WITNESSES: Mr. Peter Pomerantsev
                   Senior Fellow
                   The Legatum Institute

                   Ms. Helle C. Dale
                   Senior Fellow for Public Diplomacy
                   The Heritage Foundation

                   Ms. Elizabeth Wahl
                   Former RT Anchor
                   Freelance Journalist/Public Speaker

By Direction of the Chairman

The Committee on Foreign Affairs seeks to make its facilities accessible to persons with disabilities. If you are in need of special accommodations, please call 202/225-5021 at least four business days in advance of the event, whenever practicable. Questions with regard to special accommodations in general (including availability of Committee materials in alternative formats and assistive listening devices) may be directed to the Committee.

COMMITTEE ON FOREIGN AFFAIRS
MINUTES OF FULL COMMITTEE HEARING

Day __*Wednesday*__ Date_____*4/15/15*_____ Room_____*2172*_____

Starting Time _____*10:12*_____ Ending Time _____*11:28*_____

Recesses __*0*__ (____to____) (____to____) (____to____) (____to____) (____to____) (____to____)

Presiding Member(s)

Chairman Edward R. Royce

Check all of the following that apply:

Open Session ☑   Electronically Recorded (taped) ☑
Executive (closed) Session ☐   Stenographic Record ☑
Televised ☑

TITLE OF HEARING:

Confronting Russia's Weaponization of Information

COMMITTEE MEMBERS PRESENT:

See attached.

NON-COMMITTEE MEMBERS PRESENT:

None.

HEARING WITNESSES: Same as meeting notice attached? Yes ☑ No ☐
(If "no", please list below and include title, agency, department, or organization.)

STATEMENTS FOR THE RECORD: *(List any statements submitted for the record.)*

None.

TIME SCHEDULED TO RECONVENE _____
or
TIME ADJOURNED *11:28*_____

Jean Marter, Director of Committee Operations

HOUSE COMMITTEE ON FOREIGN AFFAIRS
FULL COMMITTEE HEARING

PRESENT	MEMBER	PRESENT	MEMBER
X	Edward R. Royce, CA	X	Eliot L. Engel, NY
X	Christopher H. Smith, NJ	X	Brad Sherman, CA
X	Ileana Ros-Lehtinen, FL	X	Gregory W. Meeks, NY
X	Dana Rohrabacher, CA	X	Albio Sires, NJ
X	Steve Chabot, OH	X	Gerald E. Connolly, VA
X	Joe Wilson, SC		Theodore E. Deutch, FL
	Michael T. McCaul, TX		Brian Higgins, NY
X	Ted Poe, TX	X	Karen Bass, CA
X	Matt Salmon, AZ		William Keating, MA
X	Darrell Issa, CA	X	David Cicilline, RI
	Tom Marino, PA		Alan Grayson, FL
	Jeff Duncan, SC	X	Ami Bera, CA
X	Mo Brooks, AL		Alan S. Lowenthal, CA
	Paul Cook, CA		Grace Meng, NY
	Randy Weber, TX		Lois Frankel, FL
X	Scott Perry, PA		Tulsi Gabbard, HI
	Ron DeSantis, FL	X	Joaquin Castro, TX
	Mark Meadows, NC	X	Robin Kelly, IL
X	Ted Yoho, FL		Brendan Boyle, PA
X	Curt Clawson, FL		
X	Scott, DesJarlais, TN		
	Reid Ribble, WI		
	Dave Trott, MI		
	Lee Zeldin, NY		
	Tom Emmer, MN		

www.ingramcontent.com/pod-product-compliance
Lightning Source LLC
Chambersburg PA
CBHW081120280526
45787CB00007B/2908